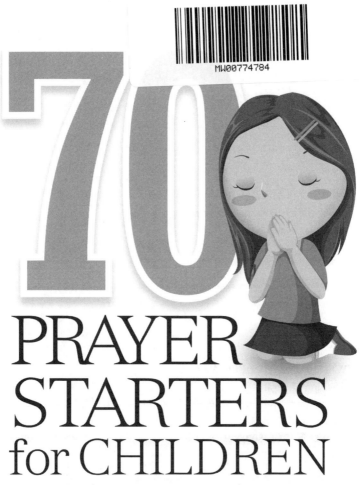

70 PRAYER STARTERS for CHILDREN

...and those who teach them

Patricia Mathson

TWENTY THIRD *23rd*
PUBLICATIONS

www.23rdpublications.com

TWENTY-THIRD PUBLICATIONS
A Division of Bayard
One Montauk Avenue, Suite 200
New London, CT 06320
(860) 437-3012 or (800) 321-0411
www.23rdpublications.com

The Scripture passages contained herein are from the *New Revised Standard Version of the Bible*, copyright ©1989, by the Division of Christian Education of the National Council of Churches in the U.S.A. All rights reserved.

ISBN 978-1-58595-840-5
Library of Congress Catalog Card Number: 2011927379
Printed in the U.S.A.

CONTENTS

Introduction

You and I were created to give praise to our God. We express our relationship with God through prayer. It is part of who we are. When we share our prayer with children and help them explore their relationship with God, we give God greater glory. So we must help children learn to pray for a lifetime. We must provide a variety of prayer experiences so they learn to pray to God in ways that speak to their hearts and their lives. We should also help families be communities of prayer, by giving them tools to help their children live in faith each day.

Prayer helps us explore God's presence in our lives and in our world. It helps us make sense of our lives and discover who we are at our core. Just as that experience is different for you and me, we must remember that it is different for children too. Individual children and families must find ways to pray so they can express their unique experience of God. By using varied forms of prayer, we invite today's children to make prayer a part of their daily lives.

This book can help children, catechists, and parents explore a variety of prayer experiences that speak to many stages and places. More than a list of activities, it will help you find approaches to praying with children and ways to help them open their minds and hearts to God. There are discussion starters to help children make prayer a part of each day. There are ideas for praying with Scripture and the Mass. While the activities are suited for ages five through eleven, they are adaptable to other ages as well. Everything is easy to do and requires a minimum of preparation.

The activities and ideas are designed for small and large groups in school and parish settings. They can also be used individually at home. It is a great resource for catechists in parish programs, teachers in Catholic schools, directors of faith formation, religion coordinators, family life ministers, leaders of lifelong faith formation, parents, grandparents, and all who want to share prayer with the children in their lives.

Each of us is called to pray with and for the next generation. In all we do, we are called to be a people of prayer. When we weave prayer throughout our day, when we share it with our children, we follow our call. Prayer brings us hope in God, hope in the future, and hope for our world today. And that is so important.

For with God, we can do all things.

CHAPTER 1

Ways to Pray with Children

Our God is an infinite God and our relationship is expressed in myriad ways. As catechists, we must help children and families express their unique experience of God. So we should be open to new ways of sharing prayer with children. Once children are comfortable with different ways to pray, they will be able to choose those that fit their relationship with God.

In this chapter, you will find a wide variety of ways to pray with children, along with tips for strengthening their prayer experiences. Vary your methods to appeal to different personalities, learning styles, maturity levels, and experiences. Be prepared for unexpected prayer opportunities that arise, such as a sunny afternoon after days of bad weather. And be sure to repeat activities that seem most meaningful to children.

ACTIVITY 1

PREPARE THE WAY FOR PRAYER

BACKGROUND

Before beginning any prayer with children, it's important to remember that transitions are difficult for them and, indeed, for all of us. Prayer is important. We must pause before beginning prayer and direct our attention to God.

WITH THE CHILDREN

Help them learn to shut out distractions by easing them into prayer. Do this by setting the scene for prayer. Avoid rushing into prayer.

Whether you are calling two children to prayer or two hundred, help them focus on the prayer before beginning. Resist the urge to use the opening words of the prayer itself, or the sign of the cross spoken loudly, as a way to quiet children for prayer. Instead, begin with words and phrases such as:

- *We gather together in prayer to remember all that God has done for us.*

- *Now we lift up our hearts and our voices in prayer to our God.*

- *Let's put ourselves in the presence of God, who is always with us.*

This calls prayer forth from the hearts of children and helps them connect with the God who is already present in their lives. Think of it as a prelude to prayer: something that helps children focus.

Try not to wait to pray when the children are getting ready to leave. Rather, make prayer a priority in the group's time together. This shows the children that you consider prayer important, and they should too.

2 HELP CHILDREN PRAY IN THEIR OWN WORDS

BACKGROUND

Children need to understand that they can bring their cares and concerns to God, who is always listening and who will always love them. They need that certainty in their lives. It is essential to give children experience in praying in their own words.

WITH THE CHILDREN

Often the best ways to help children pray are the simplest: reflecting together on the simple (and not so simple) events of their lives. Explore ways to pray to God in their lives, such as:

- give praise to God for a beautiful day
- thank God for the gift of the stars in the sky
- ask God to help us with a problem
- talk to God when we feel alone or afraid
- say we are sorry to God for what we did wrong
- celebrate when something great happens

Ask the children for their ideas about times they can pray in their own words. In this way we encourage them to talk to God about what is going on in their lives.

ACTIVITY 3 USE PRAYER STARTERS

BACKGROUND

Children need lots of practice praying in their own words. Only then will it become easier to share their thoughts with Jesus. In this way children learn to pray for a lifetime.

WITH THE CHILDREN

Give them some gentle nudges throughout their day. One way to do this is by beginning a prayer they can finish in their own words. Use any of the following starters, or make up your own:

- *God, sometimes I feel...*
- *Jesus, help me to be like you in...*
- *Father, help me to know that you...*
- *Holy Spirit, guide my life so that I...*
- *Creator God, I am thankful for...*
- *Lord Jesus Christ, I pray for...*
- *Spirit of love, be with me so I...*

The length of the prayer depends on the child and his or her needs and capabilities. For some children a one-sentence prayer from the heart is great. Older children with more writing experience can use prayer starters to write paragraph prayers.

4 ASK FOR GOD'S HELP

BACKGROUND

Life can be a challenge for all of us at times. We must help children realize that we depend on God in all things. We cannot go it alone.

Prayer gives children a sense of hope. This is one of the most important gifts we give the next generation. Some children face great difficulties, so it is important to help them understand that they can ask God for anything because God is always with them and always hears their prayers.

WITH THE CHILDREN

At every opportunity, share with children that with God all things are possible and that God is always with us. Explain often that we must ask God for help in all we do:

- We can ask God for help when we are afraid, feeling lonely, or having a bad day.
- We can pray to God when we have a difficult choice to make.

If you are comfortable, share a story with the children about a time you asked God for help. Use as much detail as you can, and tell whether you received the help you needed or if God answered your prayer in a way you did not expect.

5

GIVE PRAISE TO GOD WITH MUSIC

BACKGROUND

It has been said that when we sing, we pray twice. Music naturally appeals to children and helps them lift up their hearts to God. It reaches children in ways nothing else does. It invites them (and us) to use a God-given ability to praise our God. Music also helps children combine their voices so they praise God in community with each other.

WITH THE CHILDREN

We do not have to be great singers to enjoy music or to praise God with music. There are many ways to use music to help children pray:

- play a CD of children's praise music as they gather
- teach the children to sing a fun and upbeat song
- learn (or make up your own) gestures to go along with a song
- sing the refrain to a song from a children's hymnal as the music plays
- discuss words to a song that help us pray to our God
- listen to Christian music as they work on an activity

As they go about their day, children will sing songs they have learned. By repeating their songs of praise to God, they will find joy in singing and in being God's children. Encourage the children to sing praise to God whenever they choose. For God is always listening and always hears our prayers.

There are many collections of kid-friendly music available. Check websites of Catholic music publishers for music CDs and song books.

6 DO A CIRCLE PRAYER

BACKGROUND

Circle prayer helps children pray together in a relaxed atmosphere. It also provides another opportunity for children to learn how to pray: by listening to and observing other children.

This type of prayer is adaptable to individual situations and is especially helpful when children are worried about bad news or a tragedy in the world around them. It gives them something positive to do in these situations. Praying together in times of sorrow is another way to show children that when we turn to him, God hears our prayers.

WITH THE CHILDREN

Gather the children in a prayer circle. They can sit on chairs or the floor depending on the layout of the area. The catechist begins with an example such as, "Thank you, God, for gathering all of us together today." Then go around the circle and invite each child to say a short prayer. Another day, go around the circle and invite children to pray for an intention, such as people in need, the sick, or the homeless.

Use an object such as a heart-shaped beanbag or a small wooden cross that the children pass from person to person. Only the person holding the object speaks. This reminds children that they must listen to one another. In addition, each child knows when it is his or her turn.

Let children know that if anyone chooses not to pray aloud, he or she can simply pass the object to the next person without comment. Some children are not comfortable before a group but will try at a future time. End the prayer by praying for all the intentions that have been unsaid but that we hold in our hearts.

7

GO OUTDOORS FOR PRAYER

BACKGROUND

Sometimes a new activity improves our perspective. Change can be good for us, and a change of scenery can refresh prayer for anyone. Help children get a different slant on prayer by taking them outside to pray together.

WITH THE CHILDREN

There are many outdoor places for prayer. If you have a statue on the grounds, you can often find benches to sit on. If the grass is green, spread a sheet and have the children sit on it in a circle. If there are steps outside in the sun, sit there. Be on the lookout for alternative places to share prayer with the children.

Always be sure the children stay close to you when they are outside.

We sometimes feel closer to God outside. It is great to pray to God surrounded by the beauty of creation. Encourage children to feel the warmth of the sun on their faces and to marvel at the blue sky. Help them observe the colors of blooming flowers and listen to birds chirping. God's creation is a beautiful setting for prayer and reminds us of his presence and love in our lives. It gives us hope in God and hope in the world.

8 LEARN A SHORT PRAYER BY HEART

BACKGROUND

Memorizing a prayer means it is learned for a lifetime. When we learn a prayer by heart, we have the words to pray in our hearts at times when no prayers will come. Memorized prayer can be prayed any time and any place. No books are needed. Short prayers that are learned by heart help us pray through the day.

WITH THE CHILDREN

Choose from a short prayer, part of a longer prayer, a psalm verse, or words that speak to a child's heart. Some short prayers that even younger children can memorize include:

- *I give praise and thanks to you, O God.*
- *Jesus, be with me today and always.*
- *Lord, make me an instrument of your peace.*
- *God, may all that I do today give praise to you.*
- *Come, Holy Spirit, into my heart and my life.*

Short prayers have simple words and powerful messages. Best of all, children find them doable. They help children connect with the God who is already present in their lives and who loves them without end.

9 PRAY IN SILENCE

BACKGROUND

Silence is not easy. We often rush to fill the space. Sometimes we bombard God with our petitions and litanies of wants. But we must take time to listen. We must be open to God's presence and love. We must allow God the opportunity to speak to us:

- in the silence of our hearts
- in the words of Scripture
- in the wonders of creation
- through the actions of others

WITH THE CHILDREN

We can encourage children to listen to God speaking in their hearts and their lives. Emphasize that we must stop talking long enough to hear God's voice. If we are doing all the talking when we pray, we are not hearing God speak to us.

Explain to the children that God is calling each of us, and we must slow down and listen. This way of praying takes practice. Here is one way to get them started: Ask the children to close their eyes, say a short prayer to God, and feel God's love for them. Do this only for a minute with younger children so they can keep focused.

ACTIVITY

10 USE HAND MOTIONS

BACKGROUND

When we teach them to pray with hand movements, we help children remember their prayers. As they follow the words and actions of the group leader line by line, they enjoy the opportunity to express the meanings of their prayers.

WITH THE CHILDREN

A prayer that is wonderfully suited to hand gestures is an Act of Contrition. We can use the formal prayer, or our own words. We say to God that we are sorry for what we have done wrong and for the time we could have made a difference and did not. We ask God to help us do better in the future. God always forgives us.

My God,
   (reach toward sky)

I am sorry for my sins with all my heart.
   (hands on heart)

In choosing to do wrong and failing to do good
   (nod head)

I have sinned against you
   (push hands away)

whom I should love above all things.
   (hands on heart)

I firmly intend, with your help, to do penance,
  (bow head)

to sin no more, and to avoid whatever leads me to sin.
  (hands on heart)

Our Savior Jesus Christ suffered and died for us.
  (point to palms)

In his name may God have mercy. Amen.
  (fold hands)

Children enjoy being actively involved in prayer. Using actions with this prayer helps the children understand the difficult words and concepts. It helps them to see God as a merciful and forgiving Father.

CHAPTER 2

Pray through the Day

We are called to be people of prayer in all things. Prayer connects all areas of our lives. It is to be woven throughout our day, from the time we get up in the morning until we go to bed at night. But how can we possibly pray every moment? The answer is simple. We pray to God through our words, our thoughts, and our actions.

The methods, ideas, and activities in this chapter can help you impart this to children. You will find ideas to help them learn how to incorporate prayer into their day.

This will help you show them that prayer is an integral part of their experience. It is not something added on to our lives. Rather, it is something at our core; it helps us discover who we are as God's creation.

ACTIVITY

11

OFFER EACH DAY TO GOD

BACKGROUND

The best way to start each new day is with prayer. We give glory and praise to our God who has created us and our world. We offer all that we say and do to the Lord. We ask God's help in being open to the day's opportunities.

WITH THE CHILDREN

Invite children and families to pray together each morning at home. Share with children that just as it is important to start the day with a good breakfast, we start right when we begin by offering the day to our God. Through our morning prayer we:

- thank God for the gift of this day and the promise and opportunities it holds

- offer to God the joy and the sorrows that will come our way this day.

- ask God to open our hearts and our lives to the needs of others

Whether we pray a traditional morning offering or pray in our own words, it does not matter. Here's a prayer to pray with the children in the morning:

> *Lord Jesus, we thank you for the gift of this day and offer you all we do and say. Help us live in your light, and keep us always in your sight. Amen.*

12

GIVE PRAISE
FOR CREATION

BACKGROUND

God loves us with an unending love. God has given us a world full of wonderful things. We are still discovering new kinds of animals on the earth and new stars in the vastness of space. Encourage the children to develop a sense of wonder at our world.

WITH THE CHILDREN

Ask the children to think of some of the wonders God has made for us, such as sunshine, flowers, mountains, oceans, music, and people. Help children develop an appreciation for God's many gifts.

Children can understand thanking God for creation because they see the beauty of our world all around them. We can help them understand that there is a Creator of all life. Remind them that we are to give thanks to God for the gifts of creation and the many blessings in our lives. There is always something good for which we can give praise to our God. This is a prayer idea that will last a lifetime.

When we have a few minutes we can take a praise walk outside on a nice day or look out the window at all God has made. Help children take time to experience what is around them. Listen for birds singing in trees, and notice them flying in the sky. Touch the rough bark of a tree. See if you can find flowers blooming in the sun. Feel the wind on your face. We were created to give praise to God, who is the Creator of all that is good. Even when things are not going well for us, we can be thankful for our God who is always here with us. As the saying goes, we need an attitude of gratitude.

13

TAKE A PRAYER BREAK

BACKGROUND

Encourage the children to take time every day for prayer. Explain that a prayer break can be just enough time to say a short prayer. It does not need to be long. Neither does it have to happen at a certain hour or at the same time every day.

WITH THE CHILDREN

Share with the children how easy it to stop what we are doing at any time during the day and thank God for his gifts: sunshine after a rainstorm, the feeling of good health, the love of our families.

Ask the children to think of times when they can pray, such as when they see a bright red bird singing in a tree, when spring comes, when they hear about someone who is having a difficult time, when they are afraid, or when their day is going well.

Encourage children to discuss other times when they can pray to God. Let them know that any time is the right time for a prayer break. Follow up with the children next time you meet. Ask them if they remembered to take a prayer break and how they did it.

ACTIVITY

14 ASK FOR GOD'S BLESSING

BACKGROUND

When we ask for God's blessing, we remember that God is always with us. Blessings keep us mindful that we depend on God for all things, even life itself. Blessings help us see God's presence in our world and in our lives. We know that God is the source of all blessings.

WITH THE CHILDREN

Help the children learn to ask for God's blessing with a simple prayer, such as the following:

> *God, we ask your blessing on us today. May we live in your love and share that love with others. Amen.*

We can pray for God's blessing at many times and places. This helps us express that everything good comes from God. Encourage the children to ask for God's blessing for their lives and the lives of others. Together with the children, we can ask our God to:

- bless us and our families
- bless our day or our journey
- bless the lives of others
- bless our world
- bless us at the end of the day

We can be confident that God will hear our prayers. We know that God cares about us and loves us. We are the people of God's kingdom, and we need God's help in all that we do. Our God is an amazing God who sends us blessings each day. We must also remember to be a blessing in the lives of others.

15

OFFER PRAYER FOR OTHERS

BACKGROUND

When children are little, they pray for themselves and for their families. As they grow in faith and understanding, it is important to guide them to pray also for the needs of others. This is true for all of us—as we grow and develop, so should our prayers.

WITH THE CHILDREN

Remind the children that we are called to share God's love with others. Talk about loving others as Jesus commanded and how it means praying for their needs. Explore the idea that people sometimes experience difficult times in their lives. Whether this is the result of the actions of others or of themselves, it doesn't matter. We are to pray for them and reach out a helping hand. Encourage children to open their hearts to people for whom each day is a struggle. In this way they live in God's love.

Since its earliest days our Church has a tradition of praying for others. At Mass we pray for the needs of the community during the intercessions. We are to continue to pray throughout the week in this manner. We pray for people we know and people we do not know.

Here is another way to look at it: In this life we are all interconnected because we are all God's creation. As the people of God we are called to live in a community. Part of that relationship is praying not only for our needs but the needs of others. Another part of our relationship to the community involves asking others to pray for us.

Understanding the importance of praying for others comes gradually. The more we learn about our world and the people in it, the more we see the need for prayer. And eventually we also see that we are to put our prayers into action on behalf of other people in our world. This is what it means to live as followers of Jesus Christ.

16 LIVE IN THE HOLY SPIRIT

BACKGROUND

Jesus promised his disciples that he would send the Holy Spirit to them. He kept that promise on Pentecost. Each of us receives the gift of the Holy Spirit.

We must be open to the Spirit at work in our lives and our world. The Holy Spirit helps us to live as Jesus taught us and shows us the way to the Father. The Holy Spirit gives us the courage to stand up for what is right. Through the Holy Spirit we can walk in faith, hope, and love as disciples of Jesus Christ.

WITH THE CHILDREN

Encourage the children to pray to the Holy Spirit to help them know God's will for their lives. Let them know that the Holy Spirit will provide what we need. Jesus sent the Holy Spirit to:

- help us praise God with words and actions
- guide the choices we make each day
- open our hearts to live in love of God and others
- enable us to become all that we were created to be

Emphasize that the Holy Spirit is with us always. The Holy Spirit helps us when we gather together to give praise to God's name and when we reflect on the word of Scripture and its meaning for our lives.

The Holy Spirit brings hope. We see the Holy Spirit at work in our world where people reach out to one another in times of trouble. With the help of the Holy Spirit in our lives, all things are possible. Thus, our actions become a prayer of praise to God.

17

INVITE PRAYER IN FAITH, HOPE, AND LOVE

BACKGROUND

Prayer should always be in our hearts. We pray to God as a sign of our belief in God, who is our Father, Son, and Holy Spirit. We pray to remind ourselves to live always in the new life that we have gained through Jesus Christ.

WITH THE CHILDREN

We can share with young people how we pray in faith, hope, and love:

We pray in Faith. We should always be people of faith in our God. Our faith helps us see the evidence of God's creation. The life of Jesus shows us that it is possible to live faithfully as God created human beings to live. We are to be people who share our faith in God with others, who treat other people with dignity and respect as God's creation, and who pray in all things as Jesus did.

We pray in Hope. We always have hope because of the love and mercy of God. Even when it seems that darkness surrounds us and the way is difficult, God is with us. We can pray to God in hope at all times. We are people of hope because of the new life that Jesus Christ brings to all of us. We pray in hope because we know God is listening.

We pray in Love. We are to live in the love of God each day. We love God because God first loved us. This love is to be shared with others. It is a gift freely given to us, which could never be earned. We must reach out to other people as Jesus did and love them as we love ourselves.

Ask the children to pray for God's help to become all that God created us to be. We were made to live in faith in God, hope for the future, and love for all. Our future and our destiny are with God, and prayer is part of the journey.

ACTIVITY

18 LEARN TO PRAY AT ALL TIMES AND PLACES

BACKGROUND

Emphasize that prayer is essential. Explore with children the idea that we can pray at all times and in all places of our lives. Let them know that anytime is a good time for prayer. God is always here with us in our lives. God will always hear our prayers.

WITH THE CHILDREN

Expand children's ideas of where and when they can pray. Some children may not have experienced many different types of prayer. Ask the children to name times and places that people can pray. This helps children learn from the ideas of other children. Some answers you can expect are:

- morning and night
- inside or outside
- alone or with others
- in church or at home

Encourage the children to think of other times and places they can pray more often. Don't be shy about asking them to find more time for prayer in their lives. For instance, ask them to pray during the coming week at a place or a time when they haven't done so before. This is how they learn to pray at all times and in all ways.

19

DO A BREATHING PRAYER

BACKGROUND

We were created to share the very life of God, and breathing is a part of that life. Prayer can become part of us simply by praying as we breathe in and breathe out. This type of prayer uses the breaths we take for life to praise God, who is the Creator of all life.

Breathing prayers calm us and help us connect with God. They enable us to feel God's presence in our lives, while shutting out the distractions and concentrating on the moment.

WITH THE CHILDREN

Examples of breathing prayers are:

Come, (breathe in)
Holy Spirit (breathe out)

Lord Jesus, (breathe in)
be with me (breathe out)

This is a way to help prayer become an intrinsic part of the children. It is a new experience for many young people, but it provides another unique way for them to experience God.

20 PRAY WITH THE SAINTS

BACKGROUND

Children need heroes who model what it means to follow Jesus. It is important for children to see that prayer has always been a part of who we are as the people of God. The saints are great examples for all of us.

WITH THE CHILDREN

Tell the children stories of saints who were known as people of prayer. This gives young people examples of real people who made prayer part of their lives each day.

> Saint Monica prayed for years for the conversion of her son. She did not give up and knew that God would hear her prayers. Today we know her son as Saint Augustine.

> Saint Rose Duchesne was known by the Native American people as "The Woman Who Prays Always." She had difficulty learning their language, but she was an example of faith in God.

> Saint Therese, also known as the Little Flower, turned everything she did each day into a prayer. She prayed for others, including those who were unkind to her.

Invite the children to pray in all things as these saints did. Emphasize to the children that prayer is to be a priority in our lives. Encourage them to be people of prayer. Let the children know also that we can ask the saints to pray for us to God.

CHAPTER 3

Prayer Activities

Children learn by doing. They like to be actively involved. Prayer activities tailored to their interests, abilities, and development invite children into prayer. Use these types of activities often to make prayer more accessible, tangible, and memorable. Observe the responses of children to see which activities work.

When children are part of an activity, they see their faith in action. They can see that they are part of a community of believers. They make a connection with God in their own lives.

ACTIVITY

21

CREATE "THANK YOU, GOD" POSTERS

BACKGROUND

We can help children see God's presence and love by experiencing his creation of the world around us. Invite the children to praise God for the wonders of creation. Remind them often that our God is an awesome God who created an amazing world out of love for us.

Encourage children's interest in the world around them. The wonders never seem to end. There are many stars in space that we have not even discovered yet. On earth, there are animals in the jungle, in the desert, in the ocean, and in the sky. There are people of many different cultures who enrich our world.

WITH THE CHILDREN

Discuss with the children some of the wonders of our world. Help them name some of the things they experience in God's creation. Encourage each of them to give thanks to God for one thing in our world, such as:

- people
- flowers
- sunshine
- animals
- food

- stars
- family
- ocean
- pets
- mountains

Provide small sheets of poster board and markers. Ask the children to label their poster at the bottom with the words, "Thank you, God" and then name the part of creation for which they give thanks. On the poster they can draw a picture of what they are thankful for.

When the children have finished, ask them to share their posters with the other children if they choose to do so. Seeing other ideas can enhance their learning experience. This is also a great project for families to do at home.

22

COMPOSE AN E-MAIL TO GOD

BACKGROUND

One way to help young people learn to pray in their own words is to compare prayer with things that are familiar to them. E-mail is an example of something many children understand.

Before gathering with the children, draw a rectangle on a sheet of plain white paper to look like a computer screen. Add "To" and "Subject" lines at the top left, as the children would see when they compose an e-mail letter. Duplicate the page for each child.

WITH THE CHILDREN

Explore the idea that just as they might e-mail their friends or relatives, children can write an e-mail to God. Explain that they will use paper instead of computer screens. Walk through a few simple steps with them:

1. Write "Dear God" or "Awesome God" to start the prayer.

2. Do one of the following: thank God for something, or ask God's help with something in their lives.

3. At the end of the e-mail, they can sign "Love," and their name.

Explain that God will see the e-mail because God sees all things. This idea helps children see that praying in their own words is doable.

23

WRITE A FOUR-STEP PRAYER

BACKGROUND

When we pray we should give thanks and praise to God before rushing right in to ask God for all that we need. Children can work together to write a group prayer using the four-step prayer method. This helps children learn to pray in their own words and results in a prayer that is meaningful to them.

WITH THE CHILDREN

The four steps in writing a prayer are:

1. A greeting, such as "God," "Lord Jesus," or "Holy Spirit"

2. Praise or thanks to God for love, creation, or blessings

3. Asking for what we need for ourselves and others

4. Amen.

Go through the individual steps, and ask the children for suggestions. Write on a white board or poster board where the children can see. This helps them see what they can accomplish when they work together. When the prayer is finished, pray it together with the children. Prayers can look something like this:

Dear Jesus, we thank you for your love for each of us. Help us to share your love with others this day and always. Amen.

This makes a personal and meaningful activity at intergenerational gatherings. Each family writes a prayer together and everyone is involved. Families then take home the prayer and can say it together later.

ACTIVITY

24 COMPOSE AN ALPHABET PRAYER

BACKGROUND

Children can relate to prayers about creation since that is something they see and experience. Encourage children to write a prayer to God using the letters of the alphabet. This is an interesting, fun, and personal way for them to give thanks to God.

WITH THE CHILDREN

Let each of the children select a different letter. (This avoids comparing the work of two children with the same letter.) Children then think of things beginning with that letter for which they thank God. Give hints or suggestions to those who find this a challenge.

A child with the letter F may thank God for family, friends, food, and forgiveness. A child who chooses the letter M may thank God for mountains, monkeys, the moon, and moms. The children then use their words in writing out a prayer such as:

Dear God, thank you for all the things you have made.

Thank you for monkeys in the jungle and tall mountains covered in snow.

Thank you for the moon that shines at night.

Most of all, thank you for my mom, who takes care of me. Amen.

At the bottom of the prayer the child signs his or her name. Children also illustrate their alphabet prayers with markers. Invite the children to share their prayers with the others if they choose. Giving thanks to God has never been this enjoyable. This activity engages children in prayer and makes it personal.

25 MAKE A BLESSING BASKET

BACKGROUND

Explore the idea that God loves us so much God created an awesome world for us. It is a world of beauty if we only look around and see it. It is a world full of wonderful people who care for us. We are thankful to God for all of these blessings.

WITH THE CHILDREN

Encourage the children to talk about the many blessings God has given us. Help them think of blessings, such as families, friends, seasons, love, music, and more.

Distribute colored index cards to the children. Ask each child to write one blessing for which they are especially thankful to God. This can be something that was part of the discussion or something else the child has in mind.

Place a basket for the blessings on a prayer table where the children gather. Put a small sign near it titled, "Blessing Basket." After writing out their blessing, the children come one at a time to place their blessing card in the basket.

The basket of blessings reminds us that God loves us and cares about us. This helps the children have a positive outlook on life, and that is what we want for them. It also helps children learn from the example of others.

Encourage families to do a blessing basket at home. Suggest that family members write down blessings and place them in a basket on the kitchen table. Each time they sit down to dinner, one family member takes out a card from the blessing basket and reads it. The family then thanks God for that blessing. This is another way to encourage families to pray together.

26

MAKE GRACE PLACEMATS

BACKGROUND

Share with the children that everything in our world is a gift from God. It is God who created our world out of love for us. We are called to give thanks to God, who is the source of all good things.

WITH THE CHILDREN

Encourage children and families to give thanks to God before each meal. They can use a traditional grace before meals, their own words of thanks, or prayers from a book of graces. Tell them that we can say grace whether we are eating alone or with others. In saying grace, we remember that God gives us what we have and we are to share with others.

Help the children make grace placemats. On individual sheets of construction paper, the children write out the words to a grace before meals. For children who have difficulty writing, type these words in large typeface, print out, and copy for each child. Grace can be a simple prayer of thanks or the traditional words of grace before meals:

> *Bless us, O Lord, and these your gifts, which we are about to receive from your bounty, through Christ our Lord. Amen.*

The children glue the prayer on the paper and then add pictures of food cut from magazines or printed off the Internet.

The grace placemat can be used at home as a reminder to children and families to give thanks to God before meals.

ACTIVITY 27

CREATE SHAPE PRAYERS FOR BEDTIME

BACKGROUND

Explore with the children that we should end our day as we begin it, with prayer to our God. We should pray to God each night before we go to bed. We thank God for the gifts of the day and for being with us.

WITH THE CHILDREN

A way to pray at bedtime with young children is with shape prayers. Draw a shape such as a heart, or use a pattern from the Internet. Put the words to a short prayer inside the shape. Make four to a page, and copy on colored paper. Cut apart. Then give a shape prayer to each child to take home. They pray the prayer at bedtime, hopefully with family. Examples of shape prayers are:

- Loving others prayer inside a heart
- Thank you prayer for creation inside a flower
- Following Jesus prayer inside a cross
- Fall prayer inside a leaf outline
- Spring prayer inside a butterfly outline

The children leave the prayer near their beds for the following night. This makes prayer something tangible for them. Because their shape prayer is close to where they will be sleeping, seeing the shape prayer reminds children and families to pray at bedtime.

As they drift into sleep they can know they are in the presence of God, who is always with us and loves us with an unending love.

28

CREATE A PRAYER TREE

BACKGROUND

A prayer tree reminds us of the needs of other people and calls us to pray for them.

Encourage children to pray not only for their own needs but also for the needs of others. Emphasize that we are a community of God's people and we are to pray for one another. Discuss some of the people and groups who need our prayers.

WITH THE CHILDREN

Before gathering with the children, create a large paper tree for a wall or window. It needn't be elaborate. You can use butcher paper (crinkle it for a weathered look) to create a trunk and branches. Or simply build a mosaic tree by filling in a trunk shape with sheets of brown construction paper.

Place a sign by the tree that says, "Our Prayer Tree."

Have green construction paper and a leaf pattern available to make leaves. (You can find leaf patterns on the Internet or in teacher supply stores. Or create your own.)

Let the children cut out leaves for the prayer tree using the pattern. On each leaf they write a prayer intention such as:

- people living in poverty
- children who are hungry

- people in the hospital
- a grandparent who is ill
- victims of violence

Show them how to attach the leaves to the tree by putting tape on the back of each leaf. Let children know that they can add other intentions to the prayer tree the next time they gather. Encourage the children to pray for all the needs on the prayer tree.

29

PRAY WITH PRAYER HEARTS

BACKGROUND

Some children may not have much experience with difficult times, while others have faced many challenges. Whatever their backgrounds, we must build their awareness of others' struggles. For those who have experienced hardship, we can help them look beyond their own situation and pray for others. Stress that we pray for others at Mass and at other times too. Prayer hearts encourage children to pray for others throughout their week.

WITH THE CHILDREN

Make this simple craft by cutting out heart shapes from red copy paper. The heart is a universal symbol for love. On each heart write the name of a group in need of our prayers, such as people who are homeless, elderly, or poor. There are many, many groups of people in our world who need prayer.

Place the prayer hearts in a basket. Have the children take home a heart and pray that week for whoever is written on their heart. Having a prayer heart will help them remember to pray for others. Families can also pray for these intentions.

30

PRAY AROUND
THE WORLD

BACKGROUND

Being the people of God goes beyond nationalities and races. Each person is God's creation. Expand children's concepts of prayer by teaching them to pray for other children they do not know.

WITH THE CHILDREN

Begin by exploring the idea that the world is bigger than where they live. Display a world map as a prayer map. When the children gather, explain that you are going to learn about and pray for children of a specific country.

Choose countries that the children suggest, or nations that have been in the news due to natural disasters or ongoing poverty. Indicate the country with a star or push pin on the map. Explore the conditions in that country such as famine, war, or lack of medical care.

Then offer a short prayer for the children who live there and who need help. Ask the children to open their hearts to the needs of all people who are suffering in our world today. Include also the country where you and the children live because anyone, anywhere can be in need of prayer.

31

EXPLORE THE MEANING OF VOTIVE CANDLES

BACKGROUND

Candles fascinate children. See if your church has votive candles in addition to the candles used at Mass. Arrange to take the children to the church on a day and time when it will be open and available.

WITH THE CHILDREN

Take the children to the church to see the candles there. Explain that we light candles at Mass and at other times to remember that Jesus Christ is the light of the world and the light we are to follow in our lives.

Explain that some churches have small votive candles that serve as prayer candles. They are inside glass holders so that the melting wax and flame are contained. The donation box near the votive candles is for a contribution toward the cost of providing candles.

Let the children know that sometimes people light a votive candle and offer a prayer to God. Often it is because they face difficulties or know someone else who is. Anyone can light a votive candle.

When life is a struggle, we turn to God in prayer. We know that we need God's help in times of trouble and that God will be there for us. Our God hears our prayers and knows what we need. The flickering flame of the candle lights the darkness and brings hope to the person who has come to pray for a special intention.

Explain that when we see the lit votive candles in a church, we know that someone needs our prayers. It does not have to be someone we know. We do not need to know who lit the candle. The important thing is that we pray for people in difficult times in their lives. The votive candles show us that prayer is needed.

We are called to pray for one another. We must turn toward Jesus Christ as the light that turns away the darkness. For we are all one in our Lord Jesus Christ.

32

MAKE PEACE PRAYER CARDS

BACKGROUND

The gospel calls us to love our neighbor each day. As the people of God, we are called to live together in peace. Part of being gospel people and loving others is praying for peace in our world.

WITH THE CHILDREN

Remind the children that all people are created in the image and likeness of our God and should be treated with respect. Explain that many people in our world are victims of injustice and discrimination. We must pray for peace in our world and work for justice for all people. Peace prayer cards are a way to make this tangible for children:

1. Cut sheets of colored card stock into postcard-sized pieces.

2. At the top of each postcard put the heading "Peace Card."

3. Give each child one of the peace cards.

4. Ask each child to write on the card one way he or she can pray for peace.

Ideas might include:

- Pray for peace in our world

- Pray for peace each day
- Pray for peace for all people
- Pray that we will learn to live in peace
- Pray for peace and work for justice

Send the peace cards home with the children. Encourage them to place their cards where they will see them as a reminder to pray for peace. Stress to the children that we must not only pray for peace but also live in peace.

Let the children know that peace can begin with a single person. Together we can work miracles.

33 ACT AS PRAYER PARTNERS

BACKGROUND

This idea helps children become aware that we are all inter-connected. We are a community of God's people. We offer our prayers for the needs of others. We can ask other people to pray for our needs too.

WITH THE CHILDREN

Encourage the children to pray for other people with a Prayer Partners project. Each child prays for a partner such as:

- A homebound parish member

- An elderly patient in a care center

- A youth preparing for sacraments

- A child in another class

- A member of another family

For a large group of children, you will need to assign partner names. Be sure to have the permission of the people involved before giving out their names. While many people recognize their prayer need, it is important to respect their privacy. Sometimes a first name is all that's needed.

34

CELEBRATE WORLD DAY OF PRAYER

BACKGROUND

Each year a worldwide day of prayer is celebrated for people of many faith traditions. This ecumenical movement is an opportunity for children—and all of us—to join our voices together in prayer. We unite in praising the God of all of us and in praying for the needs of others around the globe.

WITH THE CHILDREN

The World Day of Prayer is usually celebrated on the first Friday in March. (Check a calendar to be sure.) Over 170 countries participate. Each year, a specific country is chosen to be featured, enabling the world to learn about its people, customs and traditions. The people of the featured country write the material and prayers to be used on this day, which usually includes a children's prayer service. Check online to find more resources.

On this day people all over the world lift up their hearts and voices to our God. We pray from sunrise to sunset as the earth turns toward the sun and day begins in another part of the world. What a wonderful image this is of continuous prayer throughout this day. Let families know when this international day will be held, and encourage their participation.

35

CREATE A PRAYER JOURNAL

BACKGROUND

We can help children learn a variety of ways to pray by showing them how to make prayer journals. This is a hands-on project that can personalize prayer for them. Whether they are simple with a few pages, or detailed with drawings and pictures, prayer journals can help children learn to be people of prayer.

WITH THE CHILDREN

Use spiral notebooks to help children create prayer journals of their own. Younger children can use pieces of construction paper stapled together. Following are some prayer ideas that can be included in a children's prayer journal:

- Traditional prayers to learn. The children can cut out and glue various traditional prayers in their journal, such as the Our Father and Hail Mary. These traditional prayers that are learned by heart help them pray as a community and as individuals.

- Prayers written in the children's own words. Children can also include prayers they have written as they have explored various ways to pray. These can be simple prayers written on a given theme or other prayers children have created.

- Favorite prayers that speak to their hearts. We each have prayers that we like better than other prayers.

These prayers seem to fit our lives and our experience of God. Children can choose to include prayers they like.

- Psalm verses that praise God. The words of the psalms give children and all of us words to praise our God. Help children choose short psalm verses to include as prayers. This provides yet another way to pray.

- Thank you prayers that speak of God's creation. Children write down blessings for which they are thankful. This helps them remember that all we have comes from the God who loves us.

The prayer journal can be a project for a lesson on prayer, or it can be something the children work on each time they gather. While it's a good idea to include at least one prayer of each type to give children a variety of ways to pray, there is no right or wrong way to do this and no specific order in which to do the prayers.

Encourage the children to share their journal pages with others if they choose to do so. Often that is helpful to a child who needs ideas to get started on their journal.

Invite children to illustrate the front of their journal and some of the pages inside to make it more inviting. The children can use self-stick foam stickers on the front of the journal. They can draw pictures and symbols on the prayer pages with markers.

Creating a prayer journal gives children something to prompt prayer in their lives after the group gathering.

CHAPTER 4

Pray with the Psalms

The 150 psalms developed out of people's relationship with God. Generation after generation has used the words of these ancient prayers of the Old Testament to lift up their hearts and lives in praise of our God.

There are many different kinds of psalms, but those that give praise to God are great to use for prayer. They help us express who God is in our lives and help us give thanks to God. They are prayed at Mass but can also be part of our daily prayer life. We can pray the psalms with other people, or alone.

When we pray the words of the psalms, we join our prayers with people all over the world. We pray with those who have come before us and who will come after us. We are a community of God's people that spans time.

36

GIVE GLORY TO GOD

BACKGROUND

Psalms make great prayers for the times when we come together as the people of God. The psalms give us words to give glory to God. We thank God for all that God has done for us.

WITH THE CHILDREN

Pray a joyful psalm, such as Psalm 100:1–5, with a group of children or families. This psalm helps us lift up our hearts and voices in praise of God. Part of this psalm is:

> *Make a joyful noise to the Lord, all the earth.*
> *Worship the Lord with gladness;*
> *come into his presence with singing.*
> *Know that the Lord is God.*
> *His steadfast love endures forever,*
> *and his faithfulness to all generations.*

Encourage children and families to pray the psalms at home to celebrate God's presence in our lives and our relationship with the God who created us and who is always with us.

ACTIVITY

37

DRAW PSALM PICTURES

BACKGROUND

The words of the psalms paint powerful visual images. Children give glory and thanks to God through their God-given artistic ability. Their artwork helps children express what is in their hearts.

WITH THE CHILDREN

Help the children express what a psalm means to them by drawing a picture with colorful markers. This idea helps them explore the meaning of the psalms for their own lives. Some psalm verses that are good to illustrate include:

Come and see what God has done • Psalm 66:5

Sing to the Lord a new song • Psalm 98:1

Give thanks to the Lord • Psalm 106:1

Great are the works of the Lord • Psalm 111:2

Praise the Lord, all you nations • Psalm 117:1

Display the psalm pictures where others will see them. This helps the children feel part of the community. The pictures are also a reminder to all who see them that we should give praise to God in our lives.

38

PRAY A PSALM WITH GESTURES

BACKGROUND

Gestures help children understand the meaning of the words and enable them to rejoice in being children of God. In this way children pray together to the God who loves them.

WITH THE CHILDREN

Help children pray a psalm together with gestures. The children repeat the words and gestures, so no reading is involved. Select a part of a psalm with simple words that the children can echo.

Following is Psalm 9:1–2 with gestures:

I will give thanks to the Lord
   (lift arms over head)

with my whole heart.
   (fold arms over heart)

I will tell
   (hands by mouth)

of all your wonderful deeds.
   (move hands out)

I will be glad
   (nod head)

and exult in you.
   (lift arms over head)

I will sing praise
    (hands by mouth)

to your name, Most High.
    (fold hands in prayer)

When children pray like this with their whole bodies, they are actively involved in what they are doing.

ACTIVITY 39

CREATE A PSALM CRAFT

BACKGROUND

Crafts such as this can be done in many different ways and can be dictated by the supplies you have on hand. You can adapt it in whatever way works best for the children, for you, and for the space you use.

WITH THE CHILDREN

Select a psalm verse for this project, such as:

Be still and know that I am God • Psalm 46:10

It is good to give thanks to the Lord • Psalm 92:1

This is the day the Lord has made • Psalm 118:24

Ask the children to write out the verse on paper, or copy it for them before gathering.

Have them cut out the section of the paper with the verse and citation on it. They can use scrapbook scissors to make a decorative edge.

They glue the verse to a backing, such as sheet of craft foam, construction paper, card stock, or anything you have on hand.

They decorate the verse with foam flowers, stars, stickers, seashells, pipe cleaners, buttons, or whatever is available.

Talk with the children while they work on their craft. Stress the importance of prayer and how great it is to use psalms to pray to our God. When they take their craft home, it reminds them to pray each day. In this way we encourage children and families to give thanks to God with the beautiful words of the psalms.

40

USE PSALM STARTERS

BACKGROUND

Sometimes children do not realize they can write their own prayers. Giving them a way to begin a prayer of praise invites them to do this. This personalizes the psalms for them and helps them make the psalms their own.

WITH THE CHILDREN

Encourage young people to give glory to our God each day with the Psalms. Help them write their own prayers of praise to God using Psalm verses as springboards. Suggest a phrase from a psalm, and then ask the children to finish the psalm in their own words. Some psalm phrases that can be used in this way are:

Teach me your way, O Lord... • Psalm 86:11

I give you thanks, O Lord... • Psalm 138:1

I call upon you, O Lord... • Psalm 141.1

Allow the children to take what they've learned into their lives by asking them to write down their psalms and bring them home. This way they can pray their psalm at any time or in any place they want to praise God.

41

ENJOY AN
ECHO PSALM

BACKGROUND

Psalms aren't just for older children. Young children can also use them in prayer, and reading skills aren't required when echo psalms are used. The children simply echo the words of a psalm following the lead of their catechist, teacher, or family member. This is done phrase by phrase. The children echo a few words at a time.

WITH THE CHILDREN

One psalm that can be done as an echo is Psalm 118:24. This wonderful verse reminds us that we are to rejoice in living as the children of God. Remember to pause after each line to give children time to echo the words.

This is the day (echo)

the Lord has made (echo)

let us rejoice (echo)

and be glad (echo)

This idea helps children give praise to God from their hearts. They use words that people have prayed for thousands of years but that still speak to us today.

42

DO A PSALM RESPONSE

BACKGROUND

When we use the beautiful responsorial psalm from Sunday Mass during the week, we help children make a connection between the Liturgy and their lives. It is so important to show children how we are to live what we believe.

WITH THE CHILDREN

The words of the responsorial psalm encourage us to praise our God. They give us hope that our God is a good God and is always with us.

The responsorial psalms are for all times of the Church year. The words hold universal truths about the glory of God and God's presence in our lives.

Some psalms and verses for response are:

> *Make me to know your ways, O Lord* • Psalm 25:4
>
> *The Lord is my light and my salvation* • Psalm 27:1
>
> *It is good to give thanks to the Lord* • Psalm 92:1

Check the Sunday missal, and ask children to volunteer to read various parts of the psalm. After each part all the children say the response as they praise God. In this way all the children are involved.

This provides a way for children to take responsibility for prayer. They understand that prayer is something they are to do in their lives beyond Mass. It helps them become people of prayer each day.

43

ASK QUESTIONS ABOUT A PSALM

BACKGROUND

Explore with the children what the words of an individual psalm mean to them, and to all of us. By talking about a psalm and asking questions, children begin to understand how the psalms speak to their lives. This promotes learning and prayer.

WITH THE CHILDREN

For example, in Psalm 105:1–3 we give thanks and glory to the Lord. Explore with the children what that means for them, with questions such as the following:

- What one word in this psalm jumps out at you?

- Why should we give thanks to God?

- What are some things for which we can thank God?

- How can we take care of what God has made?

- How do the words of this psalm help us to pray?

- What are ways we live out this psalm in our lives?

Be sure that the other children treat with respect each child who asks or responds. Also encourage the children to ask their own questions. Finish the discussion by inviting the children to pray psalms at other times of their lives too.

ACTIVITY

44 DISPLAY PSALM VERSE POSTERS

BACKGROUND

Another way to help familiarize children with the psalms is by making psalm verse posters that invite them to pray. Psalm posters can be done by small groups of children or by each family in an intergenerational setting. Everyone works together to make a poster with the words to a psalm verse.

WITH THE CHILDREN

Provide small sheets of poster board and markers for creating the posters. Explain that they are to print the words of the psalm verse and then decorate it with a border and artwork. Some psalms that are great for posters include:

Trust in the Lord and do good • Psalm 37:3

We will bless the Lord from this time on • Psalm 115:18

The Lord has done great things for us • Psalm 126:3

Give thanks to the Lord • Psalm 136:1

Hear my prayer, O Lord • Psalm 143:1

The psalm posters can then be displayed in a hallway or gathering area so that others will see them and remember to give praise to God.

45

LOOK UP
TITLES FOR GOD
IN PSALMS

BACKGROUND

The psalms offer different views of God to enrich our prayer experience. With a psalm activity we can help children begin to understand that our God is infinite. Explain to the children that the psalms came out of the people's experience of God. We cannot put limits on our understanding of God.

WITH THE CHILDREN

Ask children to look at some psalm verses and see what they tell us about God. Following are some psalms that portray various aspects of who God is in our lives:

> God of all nations • Psalm 47: 8
>
> God of forgiveness • Psalm 86:5
>
> God of love • Psalm 115:1
>
> God of faithfulness • Psalm 119:90
>
> God of compassion • Psalm 135:13–14
>
> God of hope • Psalm 146:5–6

Ask the young people to discuss the various descriptions of God in the psalms and the meaning of the words. These beautiful prayers give us a glimpse of who God is. Remind all who are gathered that God is greater than we could ever hope to understand.

CHAPTER 5

Pray with Scripture

Scripture is the Word of God and we are called to live it. We can and should pray with Scripture; in the Bible we see many examples of the importance of prayer in the lives of the people of God.

By his words and example Jesus showed us the importance of prayer. Scripture helps give direction and purpose to our lives as we explore what is means to live as followers of Jesus Christ.

We must pray before we read Scripture so that, with the help of the Holy Spirit, our minds and our hearts will be open. We pray after hearing the Word of God that we will live the message in our lives.

46 PRAY LIKE JESUS

BACKGROUND

In the gospels we see that Jesus was a person of prayer. He prayed at many times and in many places. The gospel accounts show us that he often went off by himself to pray. Prayer was an important part of his relationship with the Father.

Jesus prayed before he made decisions and before major events in his life. He showed us by his words and by his example that prayer is a part of who we are to be as his followers.

WITH THE CHILDREN

Ask the children to look up and discuss gospel stories about Jesus taking time to pray. Following are some verses about Jesus and prayer:

Jesus prays after feeding 5,000 people. • Matthew 14:23

Jesus prays before teaching the people • Mark 1:35

Jesus prays before choosing his apostles • Luke 6:12–13

Jesus prays for his followers • John 17:20–21

Encourage the children to pray like Jesus did. Help them think of times and places they can pray in their lives. In this way they live the gospels and follow Jesus. He shows us how we are to live.

47 RESPOND TO THE GOSPEL MESSAGE

BACKGROUND

In the gospels we hear stories of what Jesus said and did. The gospels show us how we are capable of living. Share with the young people that we must pray to live the gospel message. We were created for life with God, and praying the gospels will help us. Jesus shows us the way to the Father.

WITH THE CHILDREN

We should pray after hearing the gospels proclaimed or after reading the words ourselves. In this way we ask for the help we need to understand and live the gospel message. Here are some ideas for prayer after reading the gospel stories with children.

- Share the story of the rich man in Mark 10:17–22, and pray that we will learn to value people over things.

- Read the command of Jesus in John 13:34–35, and pray that we will open our hearts to others.

- Reflect on Jesus calming the storm in Matthew 8:23–27, and pray that we may trust Jesus in all things.

- Listen to the parable of the prodigal son in Luke 15:11–32, and pray that we will always seek God's forgiveness.

When we pray, we ask God's help to live the message of the gospels. We pray that we will become all that God created us to be. Scripture and prayer go together. Only through prayer will we be able to live the gospel message in our lives. We are called to be gospel people.

48

FRAME A PRAYER VERSE

BACKGROUND

A simple verse from Scripture sums up much of our Church teaching about prayer. Have children learn it with a craft project to actively involve them and help them remember it.

WITH THE CHILDREN

Ask the children to write or type in fancy script the following Bible verse:

Pray without ceasing

1 THESSALONIANS 5:17

Note: It is important to have the book of the Bible plus chapter and verse number so the children will remember that these words come from Scripture.

The children cut the paper a little smaller than a half sheet of paper. Have them glue this to a half sheet of construction paper.

The children make a frame for their verse by gluing colorful foam shapes such as squares, circles, and triangles around the edge. This forms the frame and draws attention to the verse.

After the gathering the children take home their verse craft and display it as a reminder to pray to God in all things. In this way we encourage children to take what they learn and live it in their lives.

49

MAKE A "FOLLOW JESUS" FOOT SHAPE

BACKGROUND

Living the gospel each day takes a lot of prayer. It shows us the way to Jesus. Explore the idea that Jesus calls each of us to follow him. Look up Matthew 4:18–22, which is the story of Jesus calling his apostles. Jesus calls us to follow him too.

WITH THE CHILDREN

This activity reminds children to ask Jesus for help on their faith journey.

Encourage children to draw around one of their shoes with a marker on a sheet of construction paper. They cut out the shoe shape around the outside edge.

Inside the foot shape, children write a prayer to follow Jesus in their lives. Talk about what they might write down. This can be something such as:

Jesus, help me to follow you each day.

Jesus, help me to love others.

Jesus, help me to forgive other people.

Jesus, help me to be a peacemaker.

Jesus, help me to share with others.

You might use this project as a bulletin board display, or you can send the foot shapes home with the children.

ACTIVITY

50 SHARE A PRAYER FROM SCRIPTURE

BACKGROUND

Jesus sent the Holy Spirit to us to help us to pray and help us to live as his followers. It is through the Holy Spirit that the Bible comes to life for us. There are prayers in the Bible that speak directly to our lives today. Help children become familiar with the words of some of the prayers in Scripture. This offers children yet another way to pray as the people of God.

WITH THE CHILDREN

Here's a beautiful prayer from the letter of Paul to the Romans that can be our prayer too:

> *May the God of hope*
> *fill you with all joy and peace*
> ROMANS 15:13

Ask the children to look up this verse in the Bible. Paul's words remind us that hope comes from our God who is the God of hope. We are to live in hope and share hope with others. Talk about what this verse teaches us.

We can personalize the words of this verse and pray it together by changing the word "you" to "us." Thus, we pray, "May the God of hope fill us with all joy and peace."

Encourage the children to pray with Scripture by using this passage, or find another that suits you.

ACTIVITY

51

DISCUSS THE OUR FATHER

BACKGROUND

Our modern version of the prayer Jesus taught us comes from Matthew 6:9–13. This beautiful prayer represents many things to us. It is a summary of the gospel. It offers us a glimpse of who God is and who we are as people created by God.

WITH THE CHILDREN

Explore the meaning of the Our Father slowly together with the young people. Here are some line-by-line discussion starters you can use:

Our Father...

This prayer calls us to faith in God who is the Father of us all. Just the first two words give us a global vision. We call God our Father. That means we know that God is the Father of all people and all nations. We are to treat people of all races and cultures with respect as God's own creation.

Give us this day...

We ask for our daily bread. We know we are dependent on God, who created all things, including the gift of life itself. We pray not only for our needs but the needs of others. We pray that all people will have food to eat and whatever they need to get through this day.

Forgive us…

> We ask God for forgiveness as we have forgiven others. We must not hold grudges or seek revenge. We must forgive those who hurt us by their words or actions. Jesus showed us this by his words and the example of his life. He forgave others.

And lead us…

> This part asks God to help us turn away from self-ishness and live as gospel people. We must resist the temptation to use angry words, to put possessions before people, and to look the other way when some-one is treated unjustly. God will hear our prayers.

Ask questions to help them review this prayer, such as:

- Why do we call God our Father?
- How should we treat other people?
- How do we honor God's name by our actions?
- What are ways to share God's love with others?
- Is it okay to hold grudges against other people?
- Why is it important to forgive others?
- Why are we to ask for God's help in our lives?

52

ACTIVITY

TALK ABOUT THE ENDING OF THE OUR FATHER

BACKGROUND

It is important that children understand why we do things. For example, the words "For thine is the kingdom and the power and the glory forever and ever" are not found in our version of the Our Father from the Gospel of Matthew. It is thought that perhaps someone copying out the gospel in the early years of the Church added these words of prayer. Thus, the versions of the Bible that used this manuscript had that addition. These words, however, were not in the manuscript that St. Jerome used to translate the Bible for us, so we do not add these words.

WITH THE CHILDREN

Talk with children and families about the different endings that some faith traditions use with the Our Father, since this can be a source of confusion when people from different churches pray together.

This is a concept older children can understand so that they are able to answer questions from others about the ending words. Explain that we use these words at Mass with the Our Father but with another prayer in between. The words are only slightly different: "For the kingdom, the power and the glory are yours now and forever." The words are a reminder of what the prayer means.

53 TRY LECTIO DIVINA

BACKGROUND

This form of Scripture study and prayer helps us reflect on the meaning of a particular Bible passage for our lives. It has been used for centuries. The Latin words *lectio divina* mean "divine reading."

WITH THE CHILDREN

Lectio divina can be kid-friendly. Here's how to adapt it for children:

- Tell the children you are going to share a Bible story with them. Invite them to listen carefully for any word or phrase that stands out for them.

- Read one of the stories from the list on the following page.

- Ask the children about the word or phrase that stood out for them. Invite them to share their word with the others.

- Ask why they think that word is important.

- Read the story again. Discuss the message for our lives today.

- Close with a prayer that asks for God's help to live the message in the Word they heard.

Try these gospel stories with the concept of lectio divina:

Blind man sees • Mark 10:46–52

Good Samaritan • Luke 10:29–37

Lost sheep • Matthew 18:12–14

Healing of the lepers • Luke 17:11–19

Storm at sea • Mark 4:35–41

Zacchaeus changes his life • Luke 19:1–10

Using this adapted form of lectio divina with children helps them learn how to read Scripture and reflect on the message in their lives. In this way they learn to listen to God speaking to them through Scripture.

ACTIVITY

54 JOIN MARY IN PRAYER

BACKGROUND

The mother of Jesus calls us to pray and gives us an example with her Magnificat, found in Luke 1:46–55. Mary proclaims this prayer on her visit to her cousin Elizabeth after the angel announces that Mary will be the mother of God. The Magnificat is an expression of Mary's faith in God. It also shows us how she lived her life.

WITH THE CHILDREN

Share a portion of this prayer with the children:

My soul magnifies the Lord
and my spirit rejoices in God my Savior,
for he has looked with favor
on the lowliness of his servant...
the Mighty One has done
great things for me, and holy is his name.

We should follow Mary's example and give glory to God by our words and our actions. We must express our dependence on God as Mary did. To remind the children, give each child a holy card with a picture of Mary. Explain to the children that Mary shows us how to pray from our hearts. We can also ask Mary to pray for us to her son Jesus.

55

COME TOGETHER WITH A PRAYER SERVICE

BACKGROUND

Young people need experience in praying together as a community of God's people. Prayer services can help, by involving all children in a group. All children participate in the responses, and they can volunteer to read or lead part of the prayer service.

WITH THE CHILDREN

Helping children create their own prayer service isn't difficult. The parts of a prayer service in order are:

1. opening prayer

2. Scripture reading

3. litany prayer

4. closing prayer

First, help them select a reading from the Bible. Focus on a particular Scripture reading. The gospels are especially good for prayer services with children.

Next, have them work together to write a litany prayer for the needs of other people. This can have a response such as "Hear us, Lord."

Finally, they can think of a short opening prayer and a closing prayer that reflects how they can live the reading. Now they are ready to go.

For example, the children can create a prayer service based on the works of mercy in Matthew 25:34–40. The children write litany prayers for people in need in our world. The opening prayer gives praise to our God, and the closing prayer asks God to open our hearts to the needs of other people in our world today.

Prayer services are also great to do with families. Invite family members to participate in a prayer service with their children. Hold the prayer service in the church or in a gathering space where there will be enough room. This is a great way to begin or end a year together, but it's also appropriate for any time in between.

CHAPTER 6

Pray through the Mass

At Mass we gather together and pray as a community to our God. We lift up our hearts and our lives to our God. The celebration of Sunday Mass connects us with God and with one another.

Our celebration of Mass is part of who we are as Catholics. The Mass reminds us of what is important in life and helps us live as followers of Jesus Christ. Through our participation in the Mass each week, we learn to have hope in God, hope in one another, and hope in the future.

56 MAKE A SYMBOL CROSS

BACKGROUND

At the beginning of Mass we come together and pray the sign of the cross. This prayer is a statement of our faith in God. It is a reminder of our baptism and who we are called to be as followers of Jesus Christ.

WITH THE CHILDREN

Share with the young people that the sign of the cross is both a prelude to prayer and a prayer in itself. We call upon God as we begin our prayer. In this way we ask God, who is Father, Son, and Holy Spirit, to be with us as we pray. The sign of the cross is:

- An act of faith in God
- A reminder to follow Jesus
- A call to prayer in our lives

This prayer reminds us that we are always in God's presence. It does not bring God into our lives but helps us remember that God is already here. The sign of the cross reminds us that we are to live each day as disciples of Jesus Christ.

Each child can make a cross with symbols as a sign of faith in Jesus Christ. First they cut out a colorful cross from craft foam. Provide patterns and scissors. Then they use self-stick Christian symbols in a variety of colors to decorate the cross. Symbols can include a heart, the word "Jesus," a small cross, or a butterfly.

The cross will serve as a symbol of their relationship with God and will recall how much God loves them. They display the cross at home as a reminder to pray each day.

57 GIVE PRAISE WITH THE GLORIA

BACKGROUND

"Glory to God in the Highest." These are the words that Luke tells us the angels sang to the shepherds in Bethlehem. We say this prayer at Mass, but it is also a prayer for our lives. The Gloria is not said or sung during Advent or Lent as we get ready to celebrate the feasts of Christmas and Easter.

WITH THE CHILDREN

Explore the words of the Gloria that speak to us of our faith in God the Father, the Son, and the Holy Spirit. Talk with the children about giving glory to God by our words and actions through the week beyond Sunday. This prayer is not an end in itself but a starting point for giving praise to God throughout the week. Help children think of ways to give glory to God in their lives. Some ideas include:

- pray each day
- treat other people with respect
- serve others in God's name
- learn about the world God gave to us
- share God's love with others
- sing a song of praise to God
- look for ways to help people in need
- praise God for creation

Through the words of the Gloria on Sunday and through our actions on the other days of the week, we give thanks to God for all that God has done for us. In this way we live what we pray.

ACTIVITY

58
DISCUSS THE FIRST READING

BACKGROUND

The first reading at Mass usually comes from the Old Testament, except during the Easter season when we read from the Acts of the Apostles. The first readings are often difficult for the children to understand but are part of our story as God's people.

WITH THE CHILDREN

Look up one of the first readings we use at Mass and discuss it. One story from the Old Testament to share with the children is that of Abram in Genesis 12:1–4. God calls Abram to go where God will show him. Share with the young people that God changes Abram's name to Abraham as a sign that Abraham was beginning a new life.

Talk about this reading and relate it to the children's lives. Ask questions about the story such as:

- What did God ask Abram to do?
- Did Abram do as God asked?
- Does God call us too?
- Is God faithful to us?
- Are we called to be faithful to God?
- Is it easy to follow God's way?
- What are things God calls us to do?

By discussing the reading, children review what it is about. They reflect on what it means for their lives. We respond to the readings by our actions and by our prayers.

There are many children's Scripture resources you can use to find ideas on other readings. In this way we enable children to make the connection between the Word of God and their lives.

59

ROLE PLAY THE GOSPEL

BACKGROUND

At Mass we hear, through the four gospels, stories of what Jesus said and did. One way to help children learn and understand gospel stories is through role play.

WITH THE CHILDREN

The children act out the story as it is read from the gospel. The children do not speak any lines. Some gospel stories that can be role played include:

Call of the disciples • Matthew 4:18–22

Blind man sees • Mark 10:46–52

Zacchaeus changes his life • Luke 19:1–10

Good Samaritan • Luke 10:29–37

Jesus and the children • Mark 10:13–16

For example, for the story of Jesus and the children, assign children to play the role of Jesus, the disciples, the children, and the adults. Allow the volunteers a few minutes to decide how they will act out this story.

Provide suggestions as needed. For instance, the adults can bring the children to Jesus. The disciples can make hand motions to send the children away, while Jesus welcomes the children by opening his arms to them.

Acting out the story helps both the "actors" and the "audience" visualize it. Better yet, they will remember it for a long time to come. Children learn best by being actively involved.

60

ACTIVITY

EXPLORE THE CREED

BACKGROUND

After hearing the readings and homily, our response to the Word of God is to proclaim our faith. We state our faith in God with the words of the Nicene Creed. The priest and the people say the Creed together at Mass each Sunday.

WITH THE CHILDREN

Explore with the young people how the Creed is divided into three sections: our belief in the Father, Son, and Holy Spirit. Explore what this means with the young people by looking up Scripture and discussing it together.

Father and Creator • Genesis 1:1–13

Jesus Christ • Matthew 16:15–16

Holy Spirit • Romans 5:5

The first section of the Creed is about God as Father and Creator of the world. Read about creation in Genesis. Ask the children to name some of the things that God has made for us, such as the sun, animals, and people.

The next part of the Creed is about Jesus Christ. The Bible story is an account of how Peter proclaims his belief that Jesus is the Son of God. Ask the children to think of things Jesus has done for us, such as showing us God's love and bringing us new life.

We then proclaim our belief in the Holy Spirit. We hear in the reading how the gift of the Holy Spirit is given to each of us. Ask the children to name some ways the Holy Spirit helps us, such as making the right choices and sharing our gifts with others.

By stressing various parts of the Creed, we help children begin to understand what we say when we proclaim this prayer at Mass. By summarizing this complicated prayer as a prayer of faith in the Trinity, we enable children to make an act of faith.

61

CREATE A THANK YOU COLLAGE

BACKGROUND

The Eucharistic Prayer is the summit of the Mass. During the liturgy of the Eucharist we offer to the Father the gift of Jesus Christ through the action of the Holy Spirit. This is the greatest gift we can give to God.

WITH THE CHILDREN

Explain that the word "Eucharist" means thanksgiving. At Mass the Eucharistic Prayer is a time to give thanks to God for all God has done for us.

Encourage them to think of things for which we can give thanks to God, such as:

- people who care about us
- food to eat and water to drink
- flowers of many colors
- amazing animals
- children of all nations
- sending us Jesus

Invite the children to make a thank you collage. At the base of a piece of heavy paper, cardboard or construction paper, they write, "Thank you, God." Then they glue on pictures from magazines of things for which they are thankful. This project helps children make a connection between the Eucharistic Prayer and their own lives. It helps them, and us, give thanks to the God who created us, loves us, and sent Jesus to us.

62

LEARN ABOUT THE LAST SUPPER

BACKGROUND

When we gather around the table of the Lord, we are united in Jesus Christ. The words of the consecration are the words of Jesus at the Last Supper he shared with his apostles. He gave us the gift of himself in the Eucharist that night.

WITH THE CHILDREN

Ask the young people to look up the story of the Last Supper in Luke 22:14–20 and read it out loud. Explain that this was the last time Jesus would gather with his disciples before his death on a cross and his resurrection. Jesus gave us the Eucharist so we would have him with us always. The Eucharist gives us the strength to live as followers of Jesus Christ.

Help them visualize this with a DVD or video about the Last Supper. (You may need to select a scene from a film about the life of Jesus to concentrate on this part.) Emphasize that the Eucharist is a gift that is freely given to us by God out of love. It is a gift we could never earn but which God shares with us. This is a special way that God shows how much he loves each of us.

The Eucharist is the gift of Jesus Christ himself present in the bread and wine for all time. In this way Jesus is with us always. Each time we come together at Mass, we share in the Eucharist and are strengthened for our faith journey to the Father, through the Son, with the help of the Holy Spirit.

63 PROCLAIM AMEN

BACKGROUND

Coming forward at Mass to receive our Lord Jesus Christ is a prayer of faith. With our Amen we proclaim that this is the body and this is the blood of Jesus Christ. We pray as Thomas did when he said to Jesus, "My Lord and my God." We are saying that we believe in all that Jesus Christ said and did.

Receiving the Eucharist unites us not only with our Lord Jesus Christ but with all people. Sharing in the Eucharist means sharing in the mission of Jesus Christ. We are to share the gospel with others. We are to serve people in need as Jesus did.

WITH THE CHILDREN

To encourage children to share the love of Jesus Christ each day, have them create signs with the words of Jesus: "Love one another as I have loved you" (John 13:34). Provide markers and paper, or print out copies of this verse before the session. Show the children how to cut out the verse and glue it to a larger piece of patterned scrapbook paper. They can decorate with heart stickers or cut hearts from another piece of scrapbook paper.

Encourage the children to put their sign where they will see it each day. Talk about where this might be, such as on a chest of drawers, window sill, or counter. This sign will help them remember to love others in the name of Jesus Christ so they can live their Amen each day.

64

BE A BLESSING TO OTHERS

BACKGROUND

At the end of Mass the priest asks God's blessing on us in the name of the Father, the Son, and the Holy Spirit. Thus, we are reminded that God walks with us in all we do. We are also called to be a blessing in the lives of others.

WITH THE CHILDREN

Help them think of simple ways to make a difference. Ideas include:

- visit someone who is lonely
- read a story to a younger child
- sit by a new child at school
- contribute items to a local food pantry
- take time to listen to someone who is sad

Distribute paper to the children, and ask them to write one way they can be a blessing to another person this week. For example, "I will be a blessing to my sister this week by playing a game with her."

If you work with the same group of children year after year, try this exercise each year, and watch how their idea of blessings grows as they grow. The concept of blessings is one for all ages and stages of life.

65

PRAY SUNDAY TO SUNDAY

BACKGROUND

When we leave Mass, we go out into the world to live Spirit-filled lives. With God's help we live what we believe. We share the good news of Jesus with others. We are called to give praise to God and serve others.

WITH THE CHILDREN

Encourage the children and families to be people of prayer all through the week. Help them see ways to do this, including:

- Take a walk together and praise God for the wonders of creation

- Say grace at dinner and thank God for food and one another

- Pray together for God's help when your family faces difficulties

- Say a special prayer on each child's birthday

- Offer prayers for people in need on the news

- Give thanks to God when you see the beauty of a sunset

- Ask God's blessing on your children before they go to bed

We know that we must live what we have celebrated. Invite the children to be people of prayer and people of service to others. Emphasize that prayer to our God is for all times and places of our lives. Prayer is not just for Sundays but for always. Sunday prayer at Mass just gets us started on our week. It is a beginning.

Help the children make the connection between the Mass and their lives. Invite them to live the Word of God each day and to look for ways to be gospel people. Encourage the children to live as disciples of Jesus Christ throughout the days of the week until we come together again at Mass.

CHAPTER 7

Send Them Forth

Here are ways to extend your teaching after you've said good-bye to the children. These include projects they can take home, and ideas for families to pray together. We should equip children to take prayer out into their lives and to make prayer a part of who they are.

You will also find ways you can continue your own work of study and preparation. We must be people of prayer ourselves before we can share prayer with others.

66 BE FAMILIAR WITH FORMS OF PRAYER

BACKGROUND

As a catechist, you are probably familiar with the five forms of prayer from the *Catechism of the Catholic Church* (#2626–43). The Holy Spirit helps us to pray in these ways. Each type of prayer expresses part of our experience of God.

WITH THE CHILDREN

It is important to be aware of all of these so you can take advantage of prayer moments with the children. Try to include all these types of prayer in planning prayer experiences for the group. This is also a great way to evaluate prayer with the group.

Blessing

Pray for God's blessing on us and our lives.

Remember that God is the source of all blessings.

Petition

Prayer is part of our relationship with God.

God hears our prayers because God created us.

Intercession

Offer prayers for our needs and for others.

We pray through Jesus to the Father.

Thanksgiving

Say thank you to God for all our gifts.

We are to give thanks in all we do.

Praise
> Give glory to God for all God is.
> Our God is an awesome God.

At some point in your catechesis, review the various prayer types so the children understand that there are many ways to pray. This encourages children to think about prayer and reminds them of the importance of prayer in their lives.

67 USE MONTHLY PRAYER INTENTIONS

BACKGROUND

Many people in our world need prayer. We are called to pray for the needs of others, even people we do not know. This is part of what it means to live as the people of God.

WITH THE CHILDREN

Encourage children and families to pray for the needs of others using monthly intentions. Varying the groups of people for whom we pray keeps our attention on the needs of others. Prayer intentions include the following:

January • refugees	July • shut-ins
February • sick	August • children
March • elderly	September • peace
April • homeless	October • missions
May • families	November • hungry
June • vocations	December • poor

Communicate these monthly intentions to families by e-mail, newsletter, parish bulletin, or on bulletin boards around your church or school. Invite families—and everyone—to pray for these intentions; this helps to cultivate your connection to families beyond your classroom.

68

MAKE A PRAYER TENT

BACKGROUND

Encourage children to pray at home by making prayer tents. This project gives the children something to take home and use for prayer.

Print or make copies of a simple children's prayer before gathering together. Be sure the prayer is short and that it appeals to children. There are many sources for children's prayers. Be sure the one you use has copyright permission. Here is one you can use:

God of love,
we thank you for being with us
in all times and places of our lives.
Help us to live as you created us,
with love and compassion for others.
May all that we do today
give praise to you.
Amen.

WITH THE CHILDREN

Give each child a half sheet of colorful construction paper. Show them how to fold it in half across the middle so that you have an 8½ x 5½ sheet. This makes a table tent that will stand up with the fold at the top. The child cuts out the prayer and glues it to the front of the table tent. Demonstrate this for the children and offer help for any who have difficulty. Then the children can decorate their prayer tents with stickers such as hearts or crosses.

The children take home their prayer tent to use alone or with their families. It is an unmistakable reminder to pray—and since the prayer is displayed prominently, there's no reason not to say it.

69

JOURNEY THROUGH THE CHURCH YEAR

BACKGROUND

As families journey through the year, invite them to follow the church's seasons and pray along the way. The varied ways to pray during the seasons celebrate who God is in our lives.

WITH THE CHILDREN

Provide children and families simple, doable ideas to pray and celebrate each season of the liturgical year. Each season offers us a unique way to pray and relate to our God. Some ways to pray the seasons include:

Advent   pray each week with the Advent wreath

Christmas   gather for prayer before a nativity scene

Lent   walk the Stations of the Cross with Jesus

Triduum   ask Jesus to show us the way to serve others

Easter   sing Alleluia to our God who brings us new life

Praying in a different way in each season allows children to explore the meaning of the seasons for their lives. Prayer helps us walk our faith journey with Jesus Christ from Bethlehem to Jerusalem and beyond.

70

PUT PRAYERS INTO ACTION

BACKGROUND

We've talked about praying in all we do. We are also called to put our prayers into action. This is an important concept to share with children. Explain that we are not just to pray for the needs of others but also to do something about it.

All of us are made in God's own image. The resources of our world were given to all of us to share. We give praise to the God who created us by the way we live our lives and how we share what we have been given.

WITH THE CHILDREN

By our prayers and actions we bring hope to the lives of other people. Here are some ways to do this:

- pray for peace and live as peacemakers
- pray for justice and work for the rights of others
- pray for the homeless and donate to a shelter
- pray for the sick and make get well cards
- pray for the hungry and give items to a food pantry
- pray for the elderly and visit a nursing home
- pray for refugees and welcome them

With God's help we are able to put our prayers into action. We must help children realize that we are to live what we pray. We are to do something about the problems and situations that are in our prayers. God sends us to make a difference in our world.